A Quick Gu...
RELATIONSHIP-BASED CARE

RELATIONSHIP-BASED CARE

Leadership

Teamwork

Evidence

PATIENT & FAMILY

Interprofessional Practice

System Design

Care Delivery

HEALING CULTURE

ISBN 13: 978-1-886624-99-3

Creative Health Care Management, Inc.
6200 Baker Rd., Suite 200
Minneapolis, Minnesota 55346 1923

CREATIVE

HEALTH CARE

MANAGEMENT

www.chcm.com
chcm@chcm.com

800.728.7766 or 952.854.9015

CONTENTS

Creative Ways to Use This Book

If Relationship-Based Care (RBC) is being implemented in your organization, it is important to understand that RBC is a comprehensive, multi-year implementation which is rolled out to the organization in "waves." That means that while it's possible you'll be among the first people in your organization to experience RBC firsthand, it's also possible that you won't have the full RBC experience for several months, or even longer. Still, the organization will begin to change in small ways that affect everyone right way.

This RBC Quick Guide will provide the orientation you'll need to engage in meaningful conversations about RBC no matter where you are in the process.

As you begin talking with your colleagues about RBC, you'll find that your organization—even if you have never before used the term *Relationship-Based Care*—will have some aspects of RBC already in place. By engaging in dialogue with others, you can appreciate the strengths that already exist in your organization, which ignites a desire to grow and develop even more qualities of a Relationship-Based Care culture.

You'll note that there is no section of this resource explicitly labeled "Patient Experience." That's because literally everything in the RBC Model is designed to improve the patient experience. The most reliable outcome of an organization's commitment to Relationship-Based Care is the advancement of a culture that feels safe, nurturing, and productive for patients, families, service providers, administrators, and clinicians in all disciplines and departments. Improved patient experience is the implicit and explicit goal of all RBC endeavors.

About Relationship-Based Care

What is Relationship-Based Care?

Relationship-Based Care (RBC) is an evidence-based model developed by Creative Health Care Management which has been implemented by organizations around the world in all types of clinical and nonclinical departments and settings. The complete model is described in the book, *Relationship-Based Care: A Model for Transforming Practice.*

Relationship-Based Care is a philosophy, an operational blueprint, and a way of being. It promotes a healing culture in health care organizations by focusing on three key relationships: the relationship with self, with team, and with patients and families.

Everything we aspire to accomplish in health care arises from how people, processes, and structures relate to one another. RBC empowers the people within organizations to align the processes and structures of care delivery with the way they intend to relate to each other as people.

Why RBC?

Because *Everyone* in Your Organization Can Positively Impact Patients and their Families

In an RBC organization, unit practice councils (UPCs) are small councils made up of first-line staff members who are empowered to improve practice in their own work areas. The story below demonstrates how people participating in a UPC have embraced their roles to create lasting changes. This story is from a U.S. Veterans Administration facility where RBC is being implemented.

Providing More Compassionate End-of-Life Care for Veterans and their Families

A unit practice council (UPC) including people from several food service departments took on the issue of having to ask the loved ones of those in hospice and other departments to pay $6 in cash if they wanted a meal. In discussing the issue, it was suggested that perhaps a Veteran services organization of some kind might be willing to provide funds to cover the costs of these meals.

The initial plan was for a representative of the UPC to send an email making the UPC's case in hopes of securing the funds, but this team had learned something about building relationships, and they knew that there was nothing as powerful as connecting in person.

Two leaders emerged from this group—two young men who had not previously thought of themselves as leaders—and they went to a meeting of representatives from local VFWs. They told their story, asked for $1,000 to cover the meals of the next 166 spouses and loved ones of dying veterans, and they got it. They advocated because they wanted to be of better service, and they put themselves forward to make it happen.

An RBC implementation leader in the organization observed, "They used to just say, 'I hate that a meal for a spouse in hospice costs $6.' That energy used to go into complaining. Now it goes into changing things for the better."

More UPC success stories will be interspersed throughout this quick guide to help you see what becomes possible when people in every department and service area in an organization are empowered to put patients and families in the center of everything they do.

Knowing Relationship-Based Care When You See It

You will know an organization has applied RBC principles when you notice:

- A caring and healing environment for everyone

- Leadership that ensures a healthy work environment and team relationships

- Effective communication and collaboration within and across departments and services

- Work allocation and patient assignments that maximize continuity of care and professional practice

- Effective ongoing system improvement initiatives

- Measurable outcomes that are openly shared as evidence that the mission and goals are achieved or that gaps exist

RBC's Fundamental Beliefs

Self-Awareness

A person's care of self and self-awareness are essential to his or her ability to care for others.

Personal Ownership for the Work

Leaders inspire a culture of ownership and accountability for excellence, visibly committing to the principle that the people closest to the work are in the best position to design care or service in their own work areas.

Commitment to Human Connection

The essence of caring is human connection. Healthy relationships among co-workers create the conditions for caring and healing of patients and families. Safe, quality care happens in the context of a therapeutic relationship between clinicians and the patients and families in their care.

The I_2E_2 Formula for Change[1]

I_2E_2 is a change management formula for creating lasting change at all levels of an organization. It is useful for every sort of change, from organization-wide change to small changes in your department or work area.

It Begins with Vision

The I_2E_2 model begins with a shared vision of what you'd like to create. No matter how large or how small the change, you'll need a clear vision of what you want to see happen in the organization or work area. If the overall change is an RBC implementation, a small interprofessional group will often craft a vision for Relationship-Based Care that incorporates the organization's existing mission, vision, and values into a vision for change that more explicitly includes Relationship-Based Care.

Inspiration, Infrastructure, Education, and Evidence

The two I's of the I_2E_2 formula are Inspiration and Infrastructure. The two E's of the formula are Education and Evidence. Inspiration, Infrastructure, Education, and Evidence will be the four main elements of your plan for change. To maximize your chances of success, attend to all four elements of your plan before embarking on the change.

Inspiration

What is the inspiration for your vision? What is it about the vision that lights people up, keeps them energized, and makes them want to participate? This is the "why" behind the whole

---

1. Adapted from Felgen, J. (2007). I_2E_2: *Leading lasting change*. Minneapolis, MN: Creative Health Care Management.

initiative. Inspiration for a Relationship-Based Care implementation will be focused on the deep satisfaction all people in health care feel when patients and families have the best possible experiences of care. Colleagues will be inspired to more active participation as they engage in a shared governance process in which their great ideas become a reality, and they see the positive impact of their work through measurable outcomes.

Infrastructure

What structures and processes within your organization's current infrastructure support the proposed vision, and what must change? Bringing your Relationship-Based Care vision to life may require changes in roles and relationships, operating principles and practices, communication processes, decision-making structures, and other structures and processes to support the work. You will likely discover that there are people in every department who are adept at redesigning infrastructure.

Education

What new knowledge or skills will people need in order to bring the vision to life? Education promotes competence, confidence, and personal commitment. Priority areas for development in a Relationship-Based Care implementation may include self-awareness, relational competence, creating therapeutic relationships with patients and families, shared governance, proactive and positive communication, critical thinking, and leadership.

Evidence

How will you know when your vision has become a reality? In the I_2E_2 formula, the term *evidence* refers to any data demonstrating that something has indeed changed—whether the vision has been fully realized or not. Evidence of success lets people know that progress is being made. Evidence also links directly back to inspiration, as there is nothing more inspiring than seeing the fruits of your labors. Clearly defined measures based on the vision should be articulated and evaluated in order to benchmark your success.

How I_2E_2 Helps Sustain the Change

As this illustration indicates, the I_2E_2 formula can and should be repeated periodically. Things can look very different six or more months down the road, and revisiting your plan for change using I_2E_2 will prove invaluable in keeping your vision a reality.

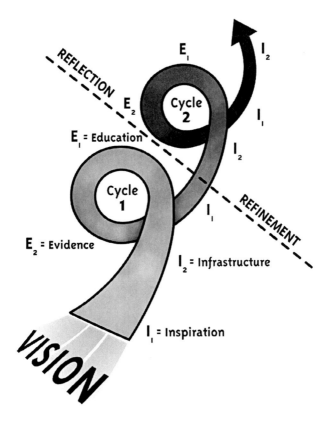

Who Can Implement Relationship-Based Care?

Everyone can.

Relationship-Based Care transforms the culture in support service departments, administrative departments, and all clinical professional departments.

Relationship-Based Care can be implemented in every department of every care setting.

An Overview of the Dimensions of Relationship-Based Care

Patient and Family

Patients and their loved ones are the reason health care organizations exist. Structures, processes, and relationships are developed to support each caregiver's ability to provide compassionate, high quality care.

In an RBC culture, caregivers, service providers, and administrators provide a compassionate presence at all times for patients, families, and each other. No matter what role you're in, an important part of your job is to learn what is most important to patients and families. All patients and families must be treated with respect and dignity by every person, every time. Human dignity is fundamental to healing, and as someone who works in any capacity in an RBC organization, it is up to you to safeguard it.

To illustrate this point, here's a story of how a member of a unit practice council changed his whole way of thinking about his work.

A UPC Success Story
RBC May Help You Redefine Your Work

A director received a letter from the son of a patient who was getting ready to go home after surgery. The patient's son wrote that he'd gotten good instructions on how to take care of his dad, but he was especially impressed with the environmental management services (housekeeping) worker who came into the room fresh post-op and saw the patient climbing into bed with fuzzy socks on. He said, "Let me get you a clean pair of socks to get into bed with; those have germs on them and you might get an infection."

Because of the invitation RBC extends to each team member, this man didn't see his job as merely keeping the environment clean; he understood that his job was preventing infection.

This happened shortly after RBC was introduced to this facility. This man was in the first implementation wave, and it was important to him to become part of a UPC so that he could impact practice. His group recently reached 100% on the organization's standard evaluation on cleanliness of the hospital environment.

The Therapeutic Relationship

The therapeutic relationship is key to keeping patients and families in the center of care. It differs significantly from social, family, or team relationships in which the needs of both people are usually seen as equally important; in the therapeutic relationship, the needs of the person receiving care are the top priority. In the therapeutic relationship, caregivers cultivate emotional safety for their patients and, when possible, for the patients' families. The purpose of the therapeutic relationship is to promote, guide, and support the healing of another person. As you can easily imagine, quality, safety, and the patient experience are all improved by therapeutic relationships.[2]

In an RBC organization, "family" is considered whomever the patient designates as family. Family members of patients often feel fear, anxiety, and uncertainty. Their own needs are sometimes overlooked, as is their potential to help patients heal. They are often wonderful sources of insight about how we can best get to know our patients' needs and cultural beliefs.

Relationship-Based Care sets the stage for families and loved ones to be our partners. We might include them more fully through things such as:

- Welcoming them through open visiting.

- Daily brief meetings with key family members to invite questions and let them know about the plan of care.

- Asking family members questions such as, "What do we need to know about your loved one to give them the best care?"

---

2. Flanagan Petry, A., Wessel, S., & Perrizo, C. (2017). Evidence that relationship-based cultures improve outcomes. In M. Koloroutis, & D. Abelson, (Eds.), *Advancing relationship-based cultures* (pp. 226-231). Minneapolis, MN: Creative Health Care Management.

- Encouraging family members to get sleep and self-care so that they can remain able to support the patient.

- Including family members, when appropriate, in the development of the patient's care plan.

Within the world of health care, the act of therapeutic connection is not owned by practitioners of any one discipline. The responsibility to offer care to another human being is something we all share.

Commitment to Patients and Their Families

We in health care are called to care for people and their loved ones during times of great vulnerability. To fulfill this sacred trust, we each commit to the following:

- I will see you as a person.

- I will give you my undivided attention when I am with you.

- I will touch you with gentleness and kindness, always mindful of your boundaries.

- I will listen to learn what matters most to you.

- I will seek to understand what this time means for you and your loved ones.

- I will involve your loved ones in your care as appropriate.

- I will help you cope and participate fully in your own health and healing.

- I will safeguard your dignity in all of my communications with you and about you.

- I will strive to create a safe haven for you and your loved ones.

- I will hold your trust in me as sacred.

Mary Koloroutis, 2017
© Creative Health Care Management

Selected Best Practices for Patient and Family Centered Care[3]

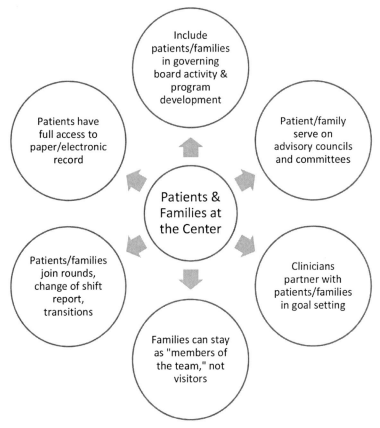

How Well Do You Currently Hold Patients and Families at the Center of Your Care?

Does your organization have a patient/family advisory committee to provide you with their perspectives as you continuously improve care and service?

---

3. Adapted from Institute for Health Care Improvement. Retrieved on March 22, 2017 http://www.ihi.org/resources/Pages/Tools/ PatientFamilyCenteredCareOrganizationalSelfAssessmentTool.aspx

Is it common in your organization or work area for clinicians, administrators, or service providers to learn about patients as people and what is most important to them? If so, how do you share what you discover with other team members?

"We experience the essence of care in the moment when one human being connects to another. When compassion and care are conveyed through touch, a kind act, through competent clinical interventions, or through listening and seeking to understand the other's experience, a healing relationship is created. This is the heart of Relationship-Based Care."

—MARY KOLOROUTIS

Healing Culture

A healing culture holds all people with respect and dignity. All are supported in reaching their full potential and are valued for their contribution to the health and healing of patients. Therapeutic relationships and a calming physical environment are core components of a healing culture.

People, Practice, and Physical Environment

The **people** entrusted to create a healing culture for patients and families are the clinicians, administrators, and service people who care for the patient and family, either directly or through others. All people in the organization must be mindful that every interaction is an opportunity to engage in a compassionate relationship. It is through the relational competence of the entire team that the culture can be a healing environment for everyone.

Our **practice** and provision of service are based on knowledge of caring theory and evidence-based caring behaviors. This includes measures that promote relaxation, comfort, and safety. Interprofessional teams are guided by professional standards and codes of ethics. Consistent and visible teamwork is essential for all involved in the provision of care and service to thrive.

The **physical environment** contributes to healing in several ways. Attention to color, beauty, quiet, cleanliness, and privacy are known to enhance the healing process. Planning for the physical space includes waiting rooms, other public areas, and staff spaces.

A Healing Culture Supports All Three Key Relationships

Relationship with Self

To stay healthy and be emotionally available for others, caregivers pay attention to their own energy levels, are self-aware and mindful as they interact, and practice self-care for body, mind, and spirit.

Relationship with Colleagues

Healthy interpersonal relationships positively impact the patient experience. All team members model mutual respect, trust, open and honest communication, and consistent, visible support.

Relationship with Patients and Families

In RBC cultures, care and services are designed to prevent unnecessary suffering including delays, physical or emotional discomfort, and lack of information about what is happening. Patients are seen, heard, and cared for as individuals.

To What Extent is Your Current Culture a Healing Culture?

Identify some of your strengths in any of the three relationships (relationship with self, colleagues, and patients and family).

Discuss the physical spaces in your organization and how they are conducive to healing. Where are areas of opportunity?

Leadership

Leadership can look a little different in an RBC organization. Relationship-based leadership includes empowering the people closest to the work to design and refine their own practice. Leaders in an RBC organization inspire and model healthy relationships. They use decentralized decision making, intentionally involving first-line staff members in decisions through a structure of **shared governance** (sometimes called shared decision making).

Leaders implement shared governance by establishing councils of staff members (unit practice councils), as mentioned earlier. These councils develop innovative changes to embed RBC into their work areas and to measure the impact of their changes. This results in staff members taking ownership for the impact of their work. Positional leaders are skilled in empowering their staff members and helping them develop leadership capabilities. When empowerment is effective, a culture of accountability and commitment emerges as staff members feel pride and ownership in the outcomes of their work.

Shared Governance

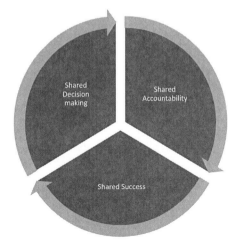

The Awesome Leadership Tool of Appreciative Inquiry

Appreciative Inquiry (AI) is a strength-based method to shift a conversation from a focus on problems to a focus on positive moments when teams and people were or are at their best.[4]

The Old Way: Focus on Problems ... Fix What's Broken

The New Way: Focus on What's Working ... Make More of It

Appreciative Inquiry (AI) conversations uncover what the organization does well. Appreciative Inquiry acknowledges best practices that are already in place and encourages people to learn from and amplify these excellent examples.

---

4. Whitney, D, Trosten-Bloom, A., Cherney, J. & Fry, R. (2004). *Appreciative team building: Positive questions to bring out the best of your team.* New York: iUniverse.

AI helps people realize that the vision for change, which may seem daunting, is achievable, and energizes people by lifting up the truth of the very good work that has been ongoing.

Using AI to Accelerate Change

Below are some examples of appreciative questions. An appreciative question is worded in such a way as to find out something positive. It may be asking someone to recount a past success or positive story.

Examples of Appreciative Inquiries

- Share a story of patient care that was especially meaningful to you—a time when your care made a difference in the life of a patient or family.

- Describe a time when you or someone you work with went the extra mile to provide a patient or family with something that mattered to them. What made it possible? What would make it possible for things like that to happen more often?

- Share a time when you knew you were emotionally present for a patient or colleague. What would it take for that to happen more often?

- Describe a time when your actions as a leader empowered staff to create an exceptional experience for patients and families and/or colleagues.

Once You Get the Hang of Asking AI Questions, You Can Ask Them Everywhere . . .

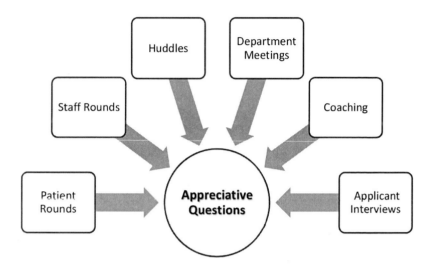

"*If you talk about empowerment, but you don't create a structure for it to happen, team members will eventually lose trust. If you offer a means by which team members can experience empowerment every day and really see their own ideas come to life, you never even have to say the word empowerment.*"

—An RBC Implementation Leader

Teamwork

Teamwork in an RBC culture requires people from all disciplines and departments to define and embrace a shared purpose and work together with trust and mutual respect. Consistent, visible teamwork is essential to the provision of high quality, safe care.

Healthy team relationships are demonstrated by the behaviors described in the *Commitment to My Co-Workers Card.*

As your co-worker and with our shared goal of excellent patient care, I commit to the following:

- I will accept responsibility for establishing and maintaining healthy interpersonal relationships with you and every member of this team.

- I will talk to you promptly if I am having a problem with you. The only time I will discuss it with another person is when I need advice or help in deciding how to communicate with you appropriately.

- I will establish and maintain a relationship of functional trust with you and every member of this team. My relationship with each of you will be equally respectful, regardless of job title, level of educational preparation, or any other differences that may exist.

- I will not engage in the "3Bs" (Bickering, Back-biting, and Blaming) and ask you not to as well.

- I will practice the "3Cs" (Caring, Commitment, and Collaboration) in my relationship with you and ask you to do the same with me.

- I will not complain about another team member and ask you not to as well. If I hear you doing so, I will ask you to talk to that person.

- I will accept you as you are today, forgiving past problems, and ask you to do the same with me.

- I will be committed to finding solutions to problems rather than complaining about them or blaming someone for them and ask you to do the same.

- I will affirm your contribution to the quality of our work.

- I will remember that neither of us is perfect and that human errors are opportunities not for shame or guilt, but for forgiveness and growth.

Compiled by Marie Manthey
© 1988, 2017 Creative Health Care Management

These common-sense agreements have been helping improve team relationships in organizations across the world since 1988. The *Commitment to My Co-Worker* statements can be used for any sort of team-building discussions. They can also be used as agreements for council and committee meetings and as behavioral standards for employee performance reviews and developmental conversations.

A UPC Success Story

Working Together to Improve a Process (and Therefore, the Patient Experience)

A pharmacy UPC looked at the issue of how bedside discharge medications were handled. Previously at discharge from medical care, the patient would have to go to the pharmacy, take a number, and wait to see a pharmacist. It was also the practice for all of the patient's medications to be renewed whether they needed them at home or not. The UPC could see that the potential for waste in their current system was high, so they instituted a change. Now, a pharmacist is on the unit Monday through Friday, and some time before discharge, the pharmacist goes into the patient's room and does medication reconciliation with the patient and family. They discuss new medications and they go over what does and does not need to be renewed. Now at discharge, the right meds are ready to go, and sometimes they get delivered to the patient.

The savings to the entire system due to cost of medications that are no longer issued when they aren't needed are currently being measured. The patients are also saving money in co-pays while experiencing increased satisfaction because their care is personalized.

How Healthy are Teams in Your Organization?

Do your recruitment and hiring practices include asking applicants to share stories about their positive interpersonal relationships?

How do you model respect for others who serve on your teams? What specific behaviors express that respect?

Interprofessional Practice

In an RBC culture, all clinical professionals are respected and valued for their unique expertise and full scope of practice. Clinical practice is grounded in research, professional standards, and ethics. "Clinical competence" is the combination of both technical and relational competence. It is accepted that the perspectives of people in multiple disciplines are essential to effective collaboration and optimal patient care and outcomes.

Clarity of Roles as a Foundation for Interprofessional Practice

The most effective way for each professional to contribute his or her expertise begins with clarity of each person's role responsibilities as well as their level of skill and knowledge.

Clarity about Delegation Choices

Licensed clinicians must be skilled at engaging team members in all disciplines and service areas to function to the full extent of their abilities. Clarity about each team member's skills, abilities, and job description is essential for effective delegation.

Clarity about Full Scope of Licensure

Effective delegation gives professionals time for the complex interventions that only they are licensed to do. Clarity of one's own role and responsibilities permits clinicians to bring their best wisdom to the interdisciplinary group, thus creating a plan for patient care that is truly interdependent and interprofessional.

Role clarity increases the confidence of everyone on the team and empowers people in all roles to participate fully.

What Does Interprofessional Practice Look Like in Your Organization?

To what extent are roles designed to allow and encourage people to work to the top of their license and/or position description, thus facilitating their most valuable contribution?

Do people in your organization know the scope of practice for each member of the team and have structures and processes in place to help determine who is best suited to meet the current needs?

"I think the extreme complexity of medicine has become more than an individual can handle. But not more than teams of clinicians can handle."

—ATUL GAWANDE

Care Delivery

Effective care delivery systems should facilitate the ability of each caregiver to know the patient as a person and to provide care based on what is most important to the patient and family. An effective care delivery system also establishes smooth transitions across care settings so that information is well communicated and the next caregivers are well prepared to receive the patient.

In Relationship-Based Care this is accomplished through a delivery system of "primary caregivers." While it's important for all caregivers to get to know patients and families as people, in a system of primary caregivers, a specific named clinician for each discipline (a primary nurse, primary physical and/or occupational therapist, primary hospitalist, etc.) accepts the responsibility for knowing the patient and family more thoroughly, developing the plan of care, and collaborating with the care team.

A system of primary caregivers enables patients and families to feel safe because they know the names of the people who are leading their care.

"Good care delivery design results in the safest possible care with the best possible outcomes while patients and families experience being held."
—SUSAN WESSEL, DAVID ABELSON & MARIE MANTHEY

Examples of Care Delivery Systems with Primary Relationships

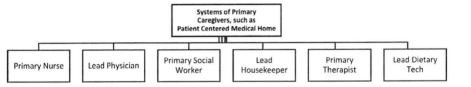

For nurses, the care delivery system of Primary Nursing has been providing patients and families with a higher level of care and human connection than is possible with any other care delivery system, since 1968, when Creative Health Care Management's founder, Marie Manthey, helped develop it at the University of Minnesota Hospital.

"Time and space are needed to develop relationships. This must be understood and considered morally valuable."
—SUSAN WESSEL, DAVID ABELSON & MARIE MANTHEY

The Three Rules of Care Delivery Design

In an RBC organization, designers of care create systems in which every subsystem, process, and structure promotes human connection. We propose the following **three simple rules** to advance Relationship-Based Care delivery design:

1. Hold the patient and family in the center of your care.

2. Make the best way the easiest way.

3. Support all relationships.

What the 3 Rules of Care Delivery Design Look Like in Action[5]

1) Hold the patient and family in the center of your care.

- Embody high care standards and ethics.

- Use respectful language that protects the dignity of patients and families.

- Design transitions that help patients feel safe and well-informed.

2) Make the best way the easiest way.

- Empower the people closest to the work to design the work.

- Make it crystal clear who's responsible for what.

---

5. Adapted from Wessel, S., Abelson, D., & Manthey, M. (2017). Care delivery design that holds patients and families. In M. Koloroutis & D. Abelson (Eds.), *Advancing relationship-based cultures* (pp. 201-220). Minneapolis, MN: Creative Health Care Management.

- Design processes and structures that minimize reliance on human memory.

- Make care coordination a priority.

3) *Support all relationships.*

- Cultivate ownership and continuity of relationships through a system of primary clinicians.

- Ensure that structures and processes support interprofessional collaboration.

- Treat the electronic health record as your electronic team member.

The clinicians and service people delivering care are in the best position to figure out how to customize care delivery processes for their patient populations within the constraints of their physical structures. If all three rules are the consistent focus, care will be safe, effective, patient centered, timely, efficient, and equitable.

A UPC Success Story

UPCs Can Have a Positive Effect on Professional Development

The Department of Operating Room Services Main OR at a surgical unit of a U.S. Medical Center consists of nine operative suites which are staffed 24 hours a day, 7 days a week. The Department is responsible for performing six different procedures for both adult and pediatric patients requiring surgical intervention within several subspecialties. The OR nursing team recognized that their current certification rate of 25%, representing just seven nurses, was one of the lowest percentages in the hospital. Acknowledging the importance of specialty certification as an organizational and national priority, the OR's unit practice council (UPC) and nursing leadership team addressed this issue with clinical nurses at staff meetings, and together they set a goal to double the number of certified nurses in the Main OR. A month later, the UPC established a goal to increase their certification rate to over 50% in 16 months.

In tandem with establishing their ambitious goal of doubling the number of certified nurses, the OR UPC conducted a needs assessment. The UPC wanted to understand existing barriers to certification for the OR staff and to generate ideas to overcome those barriers. When they learned that financial concerns and a fear of failure were the top two obstacles to certification, UPC members reached out to the Competency and Credentialing Institute, the organization responsible for the CNOR exam, to identify ways to overcome these barriers. With added support from the Department of Nursing Research and Education (NRE), the OR gathered a large group of committed nurses to take advantage of a group price discount. NRE also agreed to reimburse OR nurses who attended a certification course.

The OR UPC and nursing leadership team have sustained the momentum by including certification information and opportunities in huddle messages and at monthly staff meetings. They have promoted continued interest in the certification journey by utilizing innovative recognition strategies. When a nurse becomes newly certified, the leaders offer recognition to the individual nurse by posting his or her name on the OR unit dashboard alongside the unit's current CNOR rates. Placing this metric on the dashboard and publicly recognizing newly certified nurses helps to emphasize the importance of this initiative and encourages nurses to help the unit to achieve its goal.

This group beat its ambitious goal. Now 57% of Main OR eligible nurses are certified.

What is the Current State of Care Delivery in Your Organization?

In what ways does your organization do an exemplary job of providing a safe haven for the patient and family? What is one way in which you could improve?

How often do your patients know which physician is leading and overseeing all of their medical care? Do they know which nurse is leading nursing care for each setting? Which therapist? Which social worker, etc.? How successful are you in making patients aware of who is leading their care?

"In relationship-based cultures, compassionate care is developed, actively encouraged, and expected. Leaders model caring interactions and cultivate a community of healers in which all members of the team are seen, supported, and valued for the way their work contributes to human caring."

—Koloroutis & Trout

System Design

In RBC organizations, structures, processes, and relationships are continuously improved to bring quality, safety, effectiveness, and efficiency to patient care and the work environment. Care is taken to create effective systems. In designing any system, all resources should be maximized; these include staff time, processes of care, equipment, and funding.

Time is often our most precious resource, so our systems must be designed in a way that allows clinicians and service people to focus their time on what is most important: patients, families, and their colleagues in all disciplines. Systems need to be safe and efficient for patients, with minimal waiting and effective standards of care and service. Staff members should be supported in prioritizing their work, including determining what must be left undone.

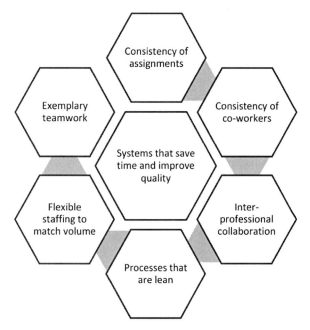

How Are Systems Designed in Your Organization?

Does your improvement process currently include first-line staff? If not, what would it take to change that?

Do any of your improvement teams include patients and/or family members?

Do you prioritize a system of consistent caregivers for patients, to save time and enable decisions based on knowledge of the patient?

Evidence

In an RBC organization, outcomes that show evidence of success are used as a source of inspiration. Measurable outcomes are identified and shared as evidence of achievement of the organization's mission and vision. Measuring the impact of RBC helps to create a supportive environment in which expectations are clear and people receive recognition for their efforts. Celebration of successful movement toward reaching our goals helps build commitment and unity within an organization.

Use of Relationship-Based Care Has Been Shown to Positively Impact:[6]

- Patient safety and clinical quality

- Patient experience

- Employee engagement and satisfaction

- Financial performance

How is Evidence Currently Used in Your Organization?

Do staff members who provide direct care and service regularly see outcome measures for their departments? Are they given the opportunity to discuss them?

Do you have effective systems of recognition and celebration for improvement in outcomes?

---

6. Flanagan Petry, A., Wessel, S., & Perrizo, C. (2017). Evidence that relationship-based cultures improve outcomes. In M. Koloroutis, & D. Abelson, (Eds.), Advancing relationship-based cultures (pp. 226-231). Minneapolis, MN: Creative Health Care Management.

A UPC Success Story

When Teams Take Ownership of their Work, the Results Can Be Breathtaking

A team member in housekeeping had this experience in his first week on the job. A patient had passed away, and this man was called to transport his body to the morgue. He was a Veteran himself, and when he walked into the room and the ceremonial flag was in disarray, he saw it as anything but ceremonial. He found another member of the housekeeping staff and asked him to help him put the deceased Veteran's body onto the stretcher. He knew that his job was simply to get this body to the morgue, but he also knew that he was working in a culture in which people mattered more than tasks, and so his extra efforts on behalf of preserving this veteran's dignity would not be seen as a waste of time or effort. He and his colleague carefully draped the ceremonial flag on the man's body, and they quietly made their way into the hallway. They walked in a very dignified way with the flag-draped body of this Veteran, spines straight, faces solemn and respectful. People in the hallway stopped what they were doing, and many of them saluted as the men passed. This was not hospital protocol; rather it was an authentic human response to the moment. A body wasn't simply being wheeled to the morgue; a human being who as a soldier had served everyone in that hallway, had died and was being treated in a manner that befitted his sacrifice. In this moment, these two housekeepers led, and doctors, nurses, and others spontaneously followed. When these two leaders got their fallen brother to the morgue, they folded the flag appropriately so that it could be presented to the man's family.

He kept up his practice of always draping the bodies of deceased Veterans appropriately and treating them with dignity, and others began to do the same. At the first possible moment, this man was given the opportunity to serve on a unit practice council, and he helped to get these practices and others instituted unit-wide. The UPC decided that every Veteran who is dying on their unit would have an angel statuette at his or her bedside. In addition, every bedside now has a small picture of the American flag. These are small gestures, but they speak volumes to patients and their families, and they also have an effect on the caregivers who come into their rooms.

We are pleased to say that stories like this one, as extraordinary as it seems, are fairly representative of the great work being done every day in organizations embracing Relationship-Based Care. This is the sort of thing people come up with when you give them ownership of their own work. RBC works because it empowers team members in every department and at every level. Through unit practice councils, the fundamental commitment team members have to the patients and families they serve is channeled into the ability to make practical changes that make a positive difference for everyone involved.

Relationship-Based Care Flash Review

Relationship-Based Care is a philosophy, an operational blueprint, and a way of being that advances the culture of health care organizations by focusing on three key relationships: the relationship with self, with colleagues, and with patients and families.

Patient and Family at the Center

Structures, processes, and relationships are developed to support each caregiver's ability to provide attuned, compassionate, high quality care. All systems and services align with patient and family needs and priorities.

Healing Culture

A healing culture holds all people with respect and dignity. All are supported in learning and reaching their full potential and are valued for their contribution to the health and healing of patients. Therapeutic relationships and a calming physical environment are core components of healing cultures.

Leadership

Leaders cultivate a shared vision, inspire and model healthy relationships, and empower the people closest to the work to continuously improve their own structures, processes, and relationships. Leaders hold patients, families, and staff members as their highest priority.

Teamwork

Teamwork requires people from all disciplines and departments to define and embrace a shared purpose and work together with trust and mutual respect. Consistent and visible teamwork is essential to the provision of high quality, safe care.

Interprofessional Practice

All clinical professionals are respected and valued for their unique expertise and full scope of practice. Clinical practice is grounded in research, professional standards, and ethics. Diverse perspectives are essential to effective collaboration and optimal patient care and outcomes.

Care Delivery

The patient care delivery system is the infrastructure for organizing care. Care is designed to allow a named primary caregiver for each discipline to accept individual ownership for the relationship, form a therapeutic relationship with the patient and family, and lead care for their discipline. Fragmented processes are replaced with systems that enable continuity of relationships and smooth transitions across the continuum of care.

System Design

Structures, processes, and relationships are continuously improved to bring quality, safety, effectiveness, and efficiency to patient care and the work environment. The perspectives of patients and the community are essential for optimizing decisions.

Evidence

Measurable outcomes are identified and shared as evidence of achievement of the organization's mission and vision. Celebration of successful movement toward reaching goals helps build commitment and unity within an organization.

What Would It Take to Bring RBC to Life in Your Organization?

What would it take for all of your patients to feel seen as individuals, with their needs heard and their preferences honored?

How might your *staff members* benefit when they create a compassionate connection with the patient and family?

How could you enhance your care delivery systems so that patients feel that the next caregivers know them as people and understand their needs?

"We are creatures of community. Those individuals, societies, and cultures who learned to take care of each other, to love each other, and to nurture relationships with each other during the past several hundred thousand years were more likely to survive than those who did not."

—DEAN ORNISH, MD

A Primary Aim of Relationship-Based Care: Improving Relational Competence

Rebalancing the Technical and Relational Aspects of Care

A care delivery system is effective when it facilitates the development of a therapeutic relationship between caregivers and patients and families. Because all of the technical aspects of health care occur in the context of human relationships, all of the technical tasks underlying the provision of care work better when we tend to relationships.

The more technically complex our health care environments get, the more important the relational aspects of care become. It isn't that relational competence is more important than technical competence; it's that it is common in health care for there to be an over-reliance/over-valuing of the technical, which is demonstrated most often by our spending an abundance of time and other resources on learning and evaluating the technical, while often neglecting the relational. RBC improves quality, safety, and the patient experience, in part by restoring that balance.

Technical expertise is a great gift, both to us and to our patients. Our relational expertise is equally a gift, both to our patients and to ourselves.

Developing and Assessing Relational Competence

In RBC, there is a competency-based framework for individual development and organizational enculturation of relational skills. The tables on these pages define and give behavioral examples of relational competencies using language from the See Me as a Person workshop (see p. 46).

Relational Core Competencies

The Relational Practice of Attuning
The practice of being present in the moment and "tuning in" to an individual or situation.

Behaviors of Attuning

Connects with the patient and family with a focus on their state of being (physical, emotional, mental, and spiritual).

Notices verbal and nonverbal cues indicating anxiety or distress, and responds appropriately.

Tunes in to the energy in the room, including one's own energy, proximity, and pace of communication.

Communicates acceptance and respect for the person receiving care through listening, spoken words, and body language.

Gives focused attention to the person and minimizes interruptions to care.

Takes appropriate action to stay tuned in to the person despite EHR or other distractions.

Conveys openness, transparency, and interest in the person.

Conveys a sturdy, compassionate, and nonjudgmental presence.

The Relational Practice of Wondering

The practice of being genuinely interested in a person. It requires an open-hearted curiosity about what can be learned about this unique individual, while intentionally suspending assumptions and judgment.

Behaviors of Wondering

Conveys genuine interest in the person receiving care.

Asks open-ended questions.

Suspends own agenda as appropriate and seeks to learn about the person.

Communicates an openness and desire to listen and learn from the patient and family.

Conveys respect for human diversity, patient and family history, and culture.

Avoids assumptions and consciously suspends judgments; is aware of potential for personal bias and refrains from labeling.

Stays open and curious to new data and information about the person.

Remembers that everyone has a unique backstory that will affect their interactions and responses to care.

Challenges oneself and one's own mindset to reflect the complete situation and experience of all involved.

The Relational Practice of Following

The practice of listening to and focusing on what an individual is teaching us about what matters most to her or him and allowing that information to guide our interactions. It involves consciously suspending our own agenda.

Behaviors of Following

Collaborates with the patient and family as involved partners in their own care.

Listens with a focus on what matters most to the person.

Refrains from interrupting, correcting, or rushing to fix things before hearing the person's perspective.

Provides care that is consistent with what the patient and family say matters to them.

Notices and responds to the person's cues and/or expressed preferences re: proximity, eye contact, touch, preferred name, etc.

Listens to and validates the person with empathetic sounds and conscious body language.

Clarifies and seeks to resolve areas of concern and/or disagreement.

Builds a sense of safety and trust by remembering specific patient and family needs and requests.

The Relational Practice of Holding
The practice of intentionally creating a safe haven to protect the safety and dignity of an individual.

Behaviors of Holding

Conveys a fundamental regard for the dignity and privacy of all persons needing care.

Acts with integrity and care by following through on all commitments.

Asks for help when necessary to meet patient and family needs.

Communicates information about the patient and family to the rest of the health care team in respectful terms and language.

Avoids derogatory labels or descriptors that may bias team members and interfere with ability to remain open and therapeutic.

Shares information and proactively attends to transitions so that the patient and family know what is happening and what to expect in their care.

Participates in and encourages consistent and visible teamwork to safeguard the wellbeing of the patient and family.

Remains a steady presence even in the face of strong emotions and crisis.

Recognizes anger as an expression of fear and distress and takes action to alleviate distress.

The Three Pillars of RBC Education

1. Re-Igniting the Spirit of Caring

2. See Me as a Person

3. Leading an Empowered Organization

Workshop
Re-Igniting the Spirit of Caring (RSC)

What is Re-Igniting the Spirit of Caring?

RSC is used by organizations to inspire and engage their entire workforce. RSC is a three-day experiential workshop that reconnects people with the joy and meaning in their work.

The *Re-Igniting the Spirit of Caring* (RSC) workshop translates the three caring relationships—care of self, care of team, care of patients and families—into daily practice, preparing everyone to model all three relationships. Here's what it looks like with a few more details.

- Body, mind, spirit balance
- Self-awareness
- Personal thriving

Care of Self

- Mutual respect; trust
- Open, honest communication
- Visible support

Care for Colleagues

- Therapeutic presence
- Learn what matters most to patient/family
- Patients as partners in decision making

Care for Patients & Families

Why Does Re-Igniting the Spirit of Caring Matter?

RSC grounds and renews members of the health care team in understanding the power and purpose of caring. Participants deepen their knowledge and skills in how to care for themselves, their colleagues, and patients and families. The RSC workshop expands hearts and minds. On the second day of RSC, former patients and families are invited to share, in small groups, their insights about caring. These insights provide best practice ideas that participants can then incorporate into their plans to implement Relationship-Based Care. Day 3 includes content on transformational leadership that inspires all staff members about their ability to be leaders of change.

Designed for all health care providers, ancillary, and support team members, RSC inspires participants to reconnect with the meaning, purpose, and joy of their work and to be even more intentional in how they can best contribute to their organization in service to patients and families.

What Participants Get from the Re-Igniting the Spirit of Caring Workshop

Comments from Leaders

"Our ICU physician participants want to make sure their whole team attends. Several physicians wish to facilitate the program."

"This was a great team-building activity for the leadership group."

"RSC played an important role in creating 'a major tectonic shift in our organization!'"

Comments from Participants

"I feel like a change has been made within me that will not only benefit me in the workplace but in life."

"Any and all opportunities to develop a sense of community among disparate units/services/departments is well worth the investment and time."

"When I first came [to RSC], I felt 'I don't need this, what a waste . . .,' but I left with new friends and a more positive attitude, and I found something I had lost: Myself. Thank you."

"I was ready to hand in my resignation . . . I had written my letter . . . and now I don't want to leave. I'm renewed!"

"This is life changing for us as caregivers—imagine what it will do for our patients and families!"

Workshop
See Me as a Person: Four Practices to Improve Quality, Safety, and the Patient Experience

What is See Me as a Person?

See Me as a Person is an exploration of four practices that improve all relationships. The therapeutic practices first appeared in the book *See Me as a Person: Creating Therapeutic Relationships with Patients and Their Families*, by Mary Koloroutis, a nurse, and Michael Trout, a child and family therapist, in 2012. Since then it has become clear that clinicians who also integrate the four practices into their lives outside of clinical settings, experience improvements in *all* of their relationships. Many RBC organizations offer the workshop that teaches these practices so staff members can more reliably apply these practices in their daily work.

"Human connection must be demonstrated continually and courageously by those to whom it comes easily, and it must be actively, compassionately cultivated in those to whom it does not."

—KOLOROUTIS & TROUT

Attuning, Wondering, Following, and Holding

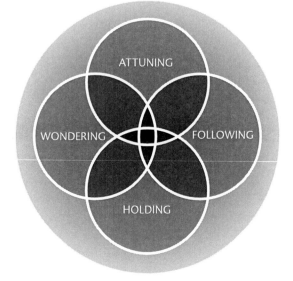

Attuning

Attuning is the foundational practice; without it, the other practices are not possible. While attuning can happen in the absence of the other three practices, the other three practices cannot happen in the absence of attuning. Unless you're "tuned in" to someone, establishing and nurturing a healthy relationship is not possible.

Attuning is the action of being present to another person; it's often explained as "meeting someone exactly where he or she is." When you tune in to someone you'll notice things about the person's way of being as well as any impact—positive or negative—that you may be having on the other person.

Wondering

Wondering is a practice of discovery grounded in curiosity and genuine interest in the other. Actively wondering prevents you from making assumptions, rushing to judgment, or disconnecting from people too quickly. You become more scientific when you wonder. Wondering helps you to resist hasty conclusions, welcome and seek new data, and imagine possible explanations beyond the apparent ones. When you wonder, you miss less and notice more.

Following

Following is the practice of allowing yourself to be informed and guided by the nuance of a person's words as much as by their content. When you follow, you allow your demeanor, words, and actions to be influenced by what you have observed about the other person. Following may mean sitting quietly for a moment with someone, offering a gentle touch, or providing what is most needed at that moment.

Holding

Holding is an act of devotion. It's a conscious decision to bring forward, affirm, and dignify that which the patient or family member has taught you, resulting in intense focus on the patient or family member while treasuring both the information and the person. You hold someone when you do what you said you'd do. You hold when you remember the things people tell you and perhaps act on them. You hold when you listen without defensiveness.

Holding is also the natural result of attuning, wondering, and following. When you do all of these things, a reliable side effect is that you create a safe haven around the person.

Why See Me as a Person Matters

The purpose of giving definition to the individual practices that comprise care is to take the mystery out of what constitutes effective relationships. Through the study of the four therapeutic practices—attuning, wondering, following, and holding—authentic connection can be learned, reflected upon, practiced, and mastered.

Everything that takes place in health care happens within the context of relationships. Imagine how your organization will change when the relational competence of everyone in the organization is improved.

What Participants Get from the See Me as a Person Workshop

"See Me as a Person is the 'how' to empathy. This is a breakthrough for me. I can now see how to teach it to my physician colleagues who struggle with empathetic connections." (Physician)

"Thank you for focusing on human connection and not the scores and scripting." (Nurse leader)

"This was a wake-up call and call to action to reignite the passion to create meaningful human connections that can assist the physical and emotional healing of our patients." (Pharmacist)

"Amazing reminder to stay present, as we always need to be." (Physician)

"I can tell the differences in nurses who have taken the workshop and those who have not." (Nurse)

"I feel closer to everyone here. I learned from everyone, and I feel better prepared to communicate with my patients." (Nurse)

Many RBC organizations offer the *See Me as a Person* workshop and/or support book groups for those reading *See Me as a Person: Creating Therapeutic Relationships with Patients and Their Families.*

Workshop

Leading an Empowered Organization: Inspiring Ownership for Excellence

What is Leading an Empowered Organization (LEO)?

In RBC organizations, it is believed that the people closest to the work are in the best position to assess, refine, and design their own processes and practices in order to bring RBC to life in their areas. For this work to go smoothly, it helps for people in all positions and departments to know some leadership basics.

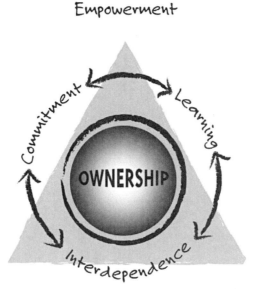

LEO prepares leaders at all levels to accept ownership for

- Building healthy interdependent teams
- Creating a learning environment where staff members reach their full potential

- Engaging everyone as committed team members who continuously improve all systems and relationships

Why Leading an Empowered Organization Matters

In an RBC organization, leadership is thought of as a quality, rather than a position. Leaders cultivate a shared vision, inspire and model healthy relationships, and empower people closest to the work to continuously improve their own work processes and relationships. Leaders hold the wellbeing of patients, families, and staff members as their highest priority.

An empowered leader demonstrates the following six core competencies that support their effectiveness.

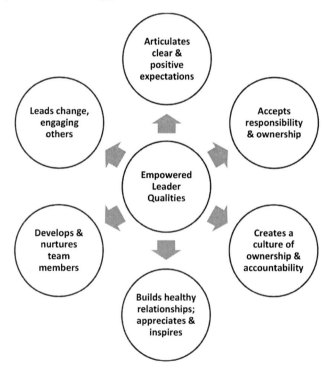

Adapted from *Leading an Empowered Organization*. Creative Health Care Management, 2015.

In a Relationship-Based Care culture, leaders create an environment of interdependence, respect, hope, and creativity—one which replaces a focus on problems with a focus on possibilities and existing strengths.

What Participants Get from the Leading an Empowered Organization Workshop

"LEO helped me recognize my areas of weakness. I will also change my language to better delegate, articulate expectations, and create a learning environment."

"The information was presented in a way that can actually be implemented. I feel like I will use everything I learned here."

"I will be clearer in articulating expectations. I will empower others to own their own accountability. I will be more open and responsive."

"I'm almost eager for a staff issue to come up . . .I finally feel like I know just what to do."

"The discussion on the techniques for assertive communication and responding appropriately when mistakes happen will be very helpful in my interactions with staff."

"I feel that this course can guide me in my future as a leader. I am very new at leading and this will really help me as I learn."

Integrating RBC into Human Resources Functions

- Recruiting and Hiring

- Onboarding

- Competency Assessment and Performance Reviews

- Succession Planning

- Coaching, Counseling, and Letting Staff Members Go

Integrate RBC into Every Phase of the Talent Life Cycle

Recruiting and Hiring

Building the best possible team to practice Relationship-Based Care includes recruiting and selecting people who fit the organization's expectations of both technical and relational competence. Job postings and position descriptions that explicitly describe people who understand the importance of relational competence and that are designed to attract people who are excited about the prospect of working in an environment in which healthy relationships are both supported and expected sifts out those who won't fit into an RBC culture and will excite and energize those who do.

Onboarding

In an RBC organization, the goal is for RBC to be expressed by every person, process, and structure therein. That means everyone in the organization must be aware of the initiative and have a basic understanding that the organization has made a commitment to improving the three key relationships (relationship with patients and families, relationship with team, and relationship with self) and to keeping patients and families in the center of everything we do. Each organization's onboarding/precepting team should take on the project of looking for every opportunity to help new employees, including students and volunteers, get up to speed with all aspects of RBC as quickly as possible.

Competency Assessment and Performance Reviews

If it's part of your job to assess competency or any other aspect of performance in an RBC organization, you have another opportunity to embed the principles and practices common to Relationship-Based Care. We are assuming that your current competency assessments and performance evaluations are already measuring technical competence and that many of them attempt to measure some relational/social skills as well. On page 56 of this booklet, more information is provided on how organizations and departments can implement RBC into their competency assessment process.

Succession Planning

Organizations typically have a protocol in place to develop leaders and provide advancement for people with leadership potential. When you become an RBC organization, the personal quality of relational competence becomes not merely a "plus"; it becomes a condition for consideration for advancement.

Coaching, Counseling, and Letting Staff Members Go

The role of leaders is to be clear about expectations and to set staff members up for success. This involves honest feedback and coaching. On occasion, employees are the wrong match for their role, or the role outgrows them. Or perhaps they are not willing to commit to being part of a culture in which healthy relationships are a stated expectation. When it's time to help transition these people out of the organization, that transition must be handled with as much love and care as we apply with those we're welcoming into the organization. How we do anything is how we do everything.

Competency Assessment: Competencies that Support RBC[7]

Infusing your organization's competency assessment strategies with the principles and practices of Relationship-Based Care (RBC) is an excellent way to reinforce the progress of individuals. Competency strategies are a great way to articulate expectations, measure outcomes, and move teams and whole organizations toward a richer expression of Relationship-Based Care. In order to be successful in using competency assessment as part of your RBC implementation, you must be aware of the key factors that make competency assessment successful. It is important to understand that competency assessment is not just about writing a competency and "checking everyone off."

To use competency assessment as a success strategy in implementing any new initiative, keep in mind that the following practices can make your competency assessment process less time consuming and far more meaningful to everyone involved.

Staff and manager collaboratively identify the competencies to be used in the implementation. This promotes joint ownership for the outcomes.

Set things up so that staff members are responsible for providing evidence of competency achievement. In an RBC culture, the manager or educator is not at the center of this process. Managers must avoid getting into the role of "checking off skills" for people. If individuals are accountable for providing evidence to the organization as it relates to their contribution to any initiative, greater autonomy is fostered and the accountability is shifted to the staff member.

---

7. Adapted from Wright, D. (2007). Competencies that support Relationship-Based Care. In M. Koloroutis, J. Felgen, C. Person, & S. Wessel, (Eds.), *Relationship-Based Care field guide: Visions, strategies, tools and exemplars for transforming practice* (pp 464-465). Minneapolis, MN: Creative Health Care Management.

Give the staff member choices in selecting verification methods for the identified competencies. Many organizations get into the rut of using two or three different verification methods. There are 11 categories of verification.[8] Become familiar with all the methods, and think about which verification methods could be used to demonstrate a competency. Consider offering two to four verification method choices for each competency identified. This incorporates adult learning principles into your competency process. You will never find one method that will meet everyone's needs. Give people choices.

Below is a sample of three competencies that reflect skills in the three key relationships in RBC:

- relationship with yourself

- relationship with your colleagues

- relationship with the patient and family

Competency	Verification Method (You would select one verification method for each competency.)
Demonstrates the ability to care for self.	**Submit** a receipt of some self-care activity that reflects a healthy self-care lifestyle. (e.g., receipt from a day at a spa, or monthly therapeutic massages, or photos from a day fishing.)
	Complete a self-care inventory that provides a self-assessment of your self-care activities, and identify two actions for self-care.

---

8. Wright, D. (2005). *The ultimate guide to competency assessment in health care.* (3rd ed.). Minneapolis, MN: Creative Health Care Management.

Competency	Verification Method (You would select one verification method for each competency.)
Demonstrates the ability to establish and maintain healthy relationships with colleagues.	**Submit** a written exemplar that shows how you used a value articulated on the "Commitment to My Co-worker©" card.
	Submit three reviews from colleagues that comment on your interactions with your team. (Suggestion for overall colleague review process: The staff member distributes three review forms to colleagues of his or her choosing, and the manager sends out three review forms to randomly selected colleagues.)
Demonstrates the ability to create a healthy therapeutic relationship with the patient/family.	**Submit** an exemplar (a written or oral story) that shows how you created or developed a relationship with a patient or family members, even in difficult situations.
	Submit a copy of a card or note from a patient or family member that reflects on some of the specifics of your care.
	Submit a copy of a section from a patient satisfaction survey that mentioned you by name in a positive way, reflecting your care of a patient and/or family.

When staff members and managers write or revise their competencies with RBC in mind, the competency process becomes part of what helps to sustain focus on RBC within the organization throughout implementation and beyond.

Relationship-Based Care as Preparation for a Magnet® Recognition Journey

The Magnet Recognition Program® and Relationship-Based Care

Your journey toward expressing RBC fully in your organization will simultaneously move you closer to being prepared to seek Magnet® Recognition and other national recognitions or awards.

For some organizations, the journey to Magnet recognition is the motivation to implement Relationship-Based Care (RBC). For others, it is the outstanding outcomes and improvements seen with RBC that lead an organization to seek Magnet recognition. Regardless of the motivation, it is important that organizations understand the role of RBC in their quest for Magnet designation. There is no doubt that the implementation of Relationship-Based Care supports the journey to Magnet designation.

In 2017 the American Nurses Credentialing Center introduced their 2019 manual with the continuous vision that Magnet organizations: " . . .will serve as the fount of knowledge and expertise for the delivery of nursing care globally . . .." This model and manual version continues with the 5 Components: Transformational Leadership; Structural Empowerment; Exemplary Professional Practice; New Knowledge, Innovations, and Improvements; and Empirical Outcomes. The following table is an overview of the expectations of a Magnet environment and how RBC can support this environment.

Model Component	Expectations of the Magnet® Environment	How RBC Can Support the Magnet® Environment
Transformational Leadership	Knowledgeable risk-takers with a strong vision.	RBC supports an environment in which transformational leadership sets the direction for data-driven best practices. RBC introduces the Transformational Leadership Cycle as a personal roadmap that supports this component.
	Participative, visible, accessible and an advocate of shared decision-making.	RBC leaders provide the inspiration and infrastructure to support staff-driven decisions to enhance patient care. RBC introduces an organizational roadmap, called I_2E_2, that supports this component.

Model Component	Expectations of the Magnet® Environment	How RBC Can Support the Magnet® Environment
Structural Empowerment	Flat, with unit-based decision-making processes; nursing active in organizational committees.	The RBC implementation is built on a shared decision-making model. *Leading an Empowered Organization* (LEO) educates and supports leaders, creating the structural empowerment seen in Magnet® environments.
	Staff voice in personnel policies and procedure development, formal peer review systems, as well as rewards and recognition programs.	The RBC infrastructure supports employee engagement through involvement in decision-making.
	Strong long-term community presence.	RBC fosters the development of care across the continuum.
	Viewed as integral to organizational success.	The nurse/patient relationship is pivotal to RBC, and therefore nursing is integral to the organization's success.
	Strong education presence and career development/advancement opportunities.	Initial and ongoing RBC education supports collaborative lifelong learning and professional development.

Model Component	Expectations of the Magnet® Environment	How RBC Can Support the Magnet® Environment
Exemplary Professional Practice	Nurses are accountable for the practice environment and are coordinators of care.	RBC is built on a theoretical framework that fosters RN responsibility, authority, and accountability (RAA) for patient care decisions. In the Primary Nurse model all care is coordinated by an RN.
	Peer support and knowledgeable experts available and utilized.	Multidisciplinary peer support is fostered through council development, communication, and reporting. Support is available through the engagement of external RBC experts.
	Autonomous practice and independent judgment are expected.	RBC facilitates the development of structures and processes that support independent patient care decisions.
	Teaching is incorporated into all aspects of practice.	RBC implementation via "waves" supports peer mentoring and teaching.
	Mutual respect and collaboration among disciplines.	The most successful RBC implementations are multidisciplinary, which leads to enhanced levels of respect and collaborative relationships to enhance patient care.

Model Component	Expectations of the Magnet® Environment	How RBC Can Support the Magnet® Environment
New Knowledge, Innovations and Improvements	Activities are considered educational, with staff participation and ownership.	RBC impacts patient care delivery through the creation of new ways of looking at old problems. These new ways lead to innovative, evidence-based practice improvements and outcomes.
Empirical Outcomes	High quality is an organization priority confirmed by outside databases.	RBC outcome measures include patient satisfaction and staff satisfaction/engagement, as well as the quantitative and qualitative data that drives practice changes.

Publishing Your RBC Story

Do you write? Creative Health Care Management has numerous outlets which may publish well-crafted stories of your organization's or department's transition to a Relationship-Based Care culture.

Journal Articles

Creative Nursing: A Journal of Values, Issues, Experience, and Collaboration has been a voice for nursing thought leaders and innovators since 1981. Sponsored by Creative Health Care Management and published by Springer Publishing Company, *Creative Nursing* is a themed peer-reviewed quarterly professional journal that welcomes submissions from people in all walks of health care. Despite its name, *Creative Nursing* is an interprofessional journal.

For submission guidelines for authors, upcoming themes, and deadlines, please contact journal editor, Marty Lewis-Hunstiger, at mlhunstiger@chcm.com.

Newsletters, Case Studies, and Books

Creative Health Care Management publishes a quarterly newsletter in which RBC success stories can be featured, and we collaborate with our clients to create case studies highlighting their unique innovations and excellent outcomes. We also nearly always have a book in the works, and we love for them to feature stories from the field. If you have a story you'd like to submit for publication in a newsletter or book, please contact developmental editor and writing coach, Rebecca Smith, at rsmith@chcm.com. If you have a story that you believe would make a good case study, please contact Ann Flanagan Petry at aflanaganpetry@chcm.com.

Your Role in Relationship-Based Care

You are playing an important role in something special. To create a new culture where relationships are valued requires everyone in the organization to be involved. You will find that the structure built to implement RBC includes clear responsibilities for everyone. Leaders must model healthy relationships, support the work of staff councils, and remove barriers to positive change, while staff members join in the creation of ideas for improvement—either by being on the staff councils or by sharing their input with their representative on the council.

This structure engages the hearts and minds of everyone in the organization. We invite you to consider what role you would most enjoy in creating a healing culture through Relationship-Based Care.

How will you use your unique skills and talents to implement Relationship-Based Care?

Creative Health Care Management
Advancing Cultures of Compassion and Love

Relationship-Based Care

Cultures of Excellence: Magnet®, Pathways Designations

Leadership Development

Re-Igniting the Spirit of Caring

Organizational Excellence

Teamwork and Engagement

Patient Experience: See Me as a Person Workshop

Staff and Physician Wellbeing

Competency Assessment

Creative Health Care Management (CHCM) is an internationally known consulting firm. Since 1978, CHCM has been partnering with health care organizations to improve quality, safety, patient experience, staff and physician satisfaction, and financial performance by improving relationships at all levels.

About CHCM

Creative Health Care Management (CHCM) is an internationally known consulting firm. Since 1978, CHCM has been partnering with health care organizations around the world to improve quality, safety, patient experience, staff and physician satisfaction, and financial performance by improving structures, processes, and relationships.

Over the last four decades, CHCM consultants have given the world Relationship-Based Care (RBC), revolutionized the field of competency assessment in health care, and provided comprehensive Magnet®[9] preparation services to organizations all over the world. Our interprofessional consultation team has partnered with health care organizations of all sizes on five continents on everything from one-day presentations to organizational and system-wide assessments, multi-day workshops, and multi-year RBC implementations and Magnet Journeys.

CHCM consultants have written and published award winning and bestselling books, including:

- *Advancing Relationship-Based Cultures*

- *See Me as a Person: Creating Therapeutic Relationships with Patients and Their Families*

- *The Ultimate Guide to Competency Assessment*

- *Relationship-Based Care: A Model for Transforming Practice*

- *A Quick Guide to Relationship-Based Care*

---

9. MAGNET®, Magnet Recognition Program®, ANCC®, Magnet®, and the Magnet Journey® are registered trademarks of the American Nurses Credentialing Center. The products and services of Creative Health Care Management are neither sponsored nor endorsed by ANCC. All Rights Reserved.

- *Competency Assessment Field Guide: A Real-World Guide to Implementation and Application*

- *Feel the Pull: Creating a Culture of Nursing Excellence*

- *Primary Nursing: Patient-Centered Care Delivery System Design*

- I_2E_2: *Leading Lasting Change*

Order CHCM's books, videos, and other products at shop.chcm.com. Volume discounts are available.

Move forward together.
Introduce your team to Relationship-Based Care.

A Quick Guide to Relationship-Based Care is a simple way for you to invite everyone in your organization into your culture advancement initiative.

No matter where you are in your RBC implementation, this concise, inspirational resource will help everyone in your organization participate meaningfully in your Relationship-Based Care journey from day-one.

Contact your client manager or CHCM today to order copies of this valuable resource for every person in your organization or to learn more about how to advance Relationship-Based Care in your unique health care setting!

800.728.7766 • CHCM.com

ADVANCING RELATIONSHIP-BASED CULTURES

Softcover, 356 pages (2017)
Retail: $34.95

Softcover ISBN: 978-1-886624-97-9
e-book ISBN: 978-1-886624-98-6
Audiobook ISBN: 978-1-518991-48-6

To purchase visit: shop.CHCM.com

Also available from CHCM

Everything in health care works better when all relationships are healthy.

This award-winning book advances the ongoing conversation about what it will take to create the best possible health care system. Through these important conversations, individuals and teams in all disciplines and roles will

- Rediscover shared purpose
- Renew reverence for the work of human caring
- Appreciate the confluence of relational and clinical competence that advances relationship-based healing cultures

Advancing Relationship-Based Cultures provides a practical how-to for the creation and nurturance of healthy relationships in health care. Readers will understand that when you empower people, giving them the tools to take excellent care of themselves, one another, and the patients and families in their care, organizations thrive.

Please visit: CHCM.com

CREATIVE

HEALTH CARE

MANAGEMENT